HOW
THE UNIVERSE
BEGAN

HOW THE UNIVERSE BEGAN

by William Jaspersohn

illustrated by Anthony Accardo

Franklin Watts   New York/London/Toronto/Sydney   1985

Library of Congress Cataloging in Publication Data

Jaspersohn, William.
  How the universe began.

  Summary: Explains in simple terms how the
universe began with the "big bang theory." Also de-
scribes the formation of the stars, planets, and our
Solar System.
  1. Cosmology—Juvenile literature.[1. Cosmology. 2. Universe] I. Accardo, Anthony, ill. II. Title
  QB983.J37 1985   523.1   85-10545
  ISBN 0-531-10032-4

For ANDREW,
born of this universe,
and for
VIRTUE and VIRTUE'S EMILY

On a clear night,
look out your window.
What do you see?
Overhead, billions of stars
burn and twinkle like
bright chips in the black sky.
Our own planet, Earth,
is just one small speck in
this vast sea of stars.
We call this huge, huge collection
of stars and planets
the *universe*.
But have you ever wondered where
all the stars and planets came from?
Or how old the universe is?
Or how it all began?

Sky scientists, called
astronomers, have studied
the heavens for years.
They are not sure *exactly*
how the universe began,
but they do have some good ideas.
In science, such ideas
are called *theories*.
One theory of how the universe began
is called the *big bang theory*.
It is the theory
that astronomers like the most.
To understand
the big bang theory of the universe,
let us go back in time
some 20,000,000,000 years.
(That's twenty billion years!)

Twenty billion years ago
there were no stars.
There were no planets.
There was no Sun.
There was no Earth.

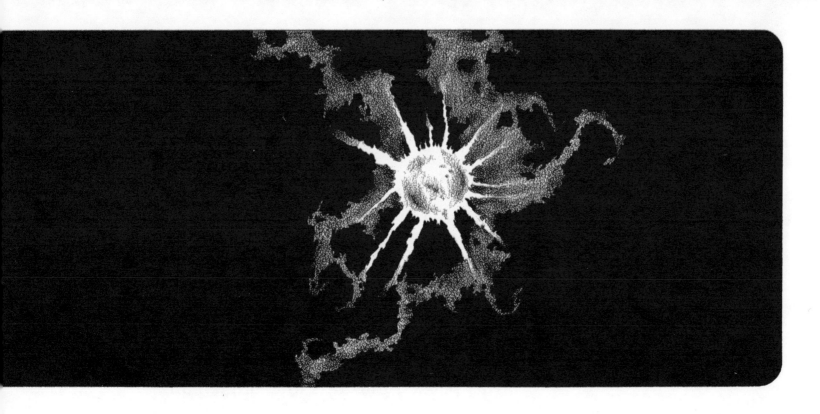

There was no Moon.
There was nothing.
Just a strange ball of stuff,
thick and hot,
known as *matter*.

No one knows
how big this strange ball was,
or how it was made,
or where it came from.
But many astronomers believe
that all the energy of the universe
was packed into this one single ball.

Then, suddenly and without warning,
the ball exploded. The light was blinding.
The heat was tremendous—
more than ten billion degrees!
Matter, along with energy called *radiation*,
flew outward in all directions.

In one fiery burst
the universe was born.
It must have been something to see,
that explosion.
It must have been scary
and beautiful.

For the next
three hundred thousand years,
the matter and radiation spread
evenly outward.
The universe lay blanketed
in a thick, hot fog.
But slowly, as time passed,
this fog of matter and
radiation cooled.
And as it did,
wondrous things started to happen.

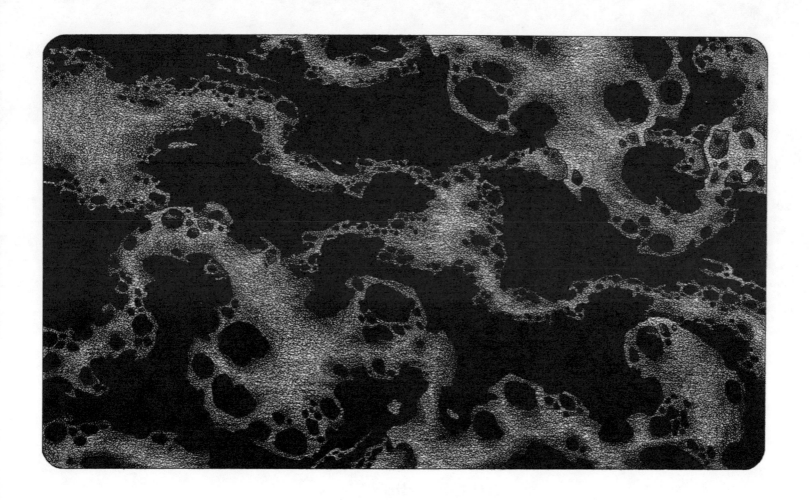

A simple gas formed
from the cooling explosion.
This was *hydrogen*,
the building block
of the universe.

Blobs of hydrogen mixed with dust
and formed clouds called
protogalactic clouds.
These clouds were huge—
trillions and trillions of miles wide.

Some astronomers think that
as the clouds swirled,
they shrank.
They broke and formed
smaller clouds called
galaxies.
Some galaxies were pancake-shaped.

Astronomers call these *ellipticals*.
Others looked like pinwheels.
These are called *spiral galaxies*.
They were all enormous—
still trillions of miles wide.
It was in these slowly spinning galaxies
that the first stars were born.

The stars came this way:
Gas in the galaxies
kept cooling.
The cooled gas broke
into blobs called
dark globules.
These globules were very wobbly.
They couldn't keep from shrinking.
Their insides got squeezed
tighter and tighter.

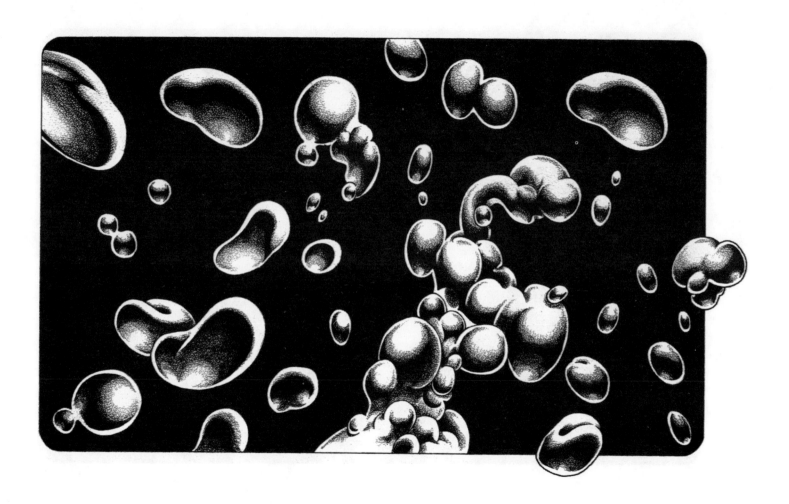

As each globule squeezed tight,
its middle got hot.
It glowed in space like
a huge hunk of charcoal.
In time, the globules got
so hot and so bright,
you couldn't look at them.
Four billion years
after the big bang explosion,
the first stars were born
from dark globules.

Sometimes galaxies crashed
into each other.
New stars were born
from the smashup.
These early stars did something important.
They served as chemical
factories for the different galaxies.

The smaller stars
made carbon and oxygen
as they burned.
The larger stars made
heavy metals,
such as iron, gold, and
uranium.

One by one,
over billions of years,
these stars exploded.
They showered their galaxies
with metals and chemicals.
Astronomers call
these smaller exploding stars
novas.
They call the larger exploding stars
supernovas.
Astronomers think that all
the basic metals and all
the basic chemicals in the
universe emerged from
these novas and supernovas.

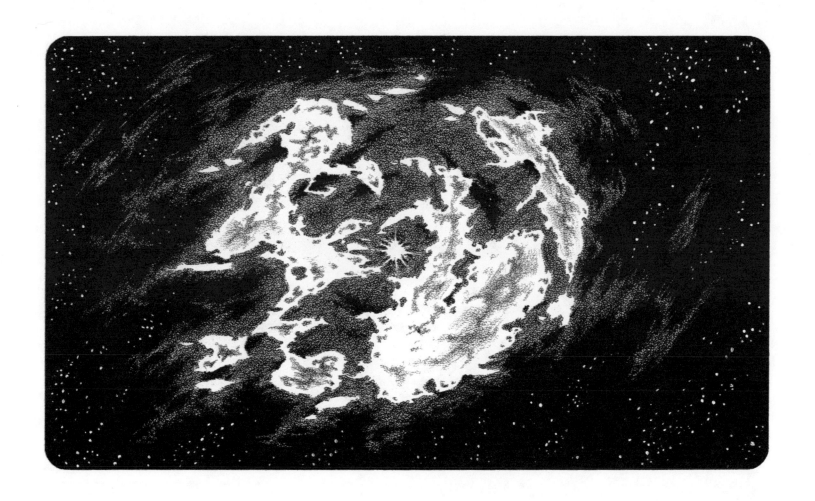

Do you know what that means?
It means that
every atom in your body—
the iron in your blood,
the calcium in your bones,
the oxygen that you breathe—
was made long ago
inside stars.
So was everything else
in this world.
Can you believe it?
We are actually made
of old stars!

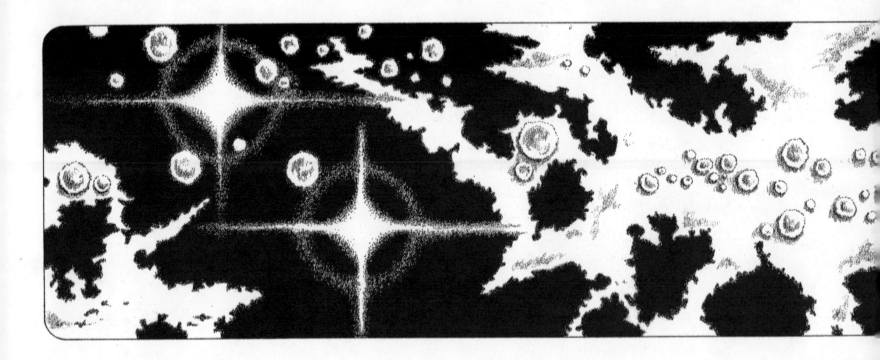

But what happened next
in the creation of the universe?
The rubble from the
supernova explosions
spread through the galaxies
as massive clouds of
dust and gas.

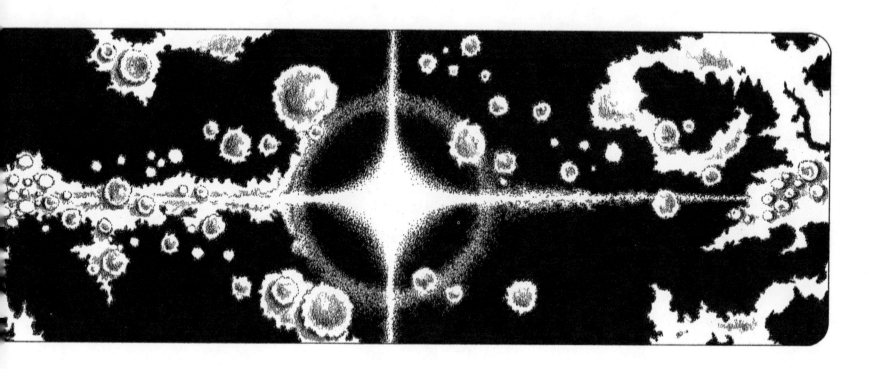

New stars formed
from these rich, dusty clouds—
smaller stars, with longer life spans.
Billions of years passed
as more stars were born.
The universe was now
about fifteen billion years old.

At the edge of one galaxy,
known as the Milky Way,
the dusty leftovers of a
supernova explosion
slowly swirled.
For us, this was an important
dust cloud.
Why? Because from this cloud
of metals, chemicals, and gases
came our Sun, our Earth, and
eight other planets.

How did this happen?
Many astronomers think
that the force from a
nearby supernova explosion
sent a shock wave
through the dust cloud.
This made the cloud
spin faster and faster.
The spinning cloud began
to shrink.
The shrinking cloud
formed a core, thick and hot.
This would become
the Sun that warms us.

Meanwhile,
outside the hot core,
the other dust and gases
began to cool.
Bits of dust formed icy grains.
The dust grains then spun
into a huge, flat ring
around the hot core.
The ring kept spinning.
As the ring spun,
the icy dust grains began
bumping into each other and
lumping together.
The more the lumps bumped,
the bigger they grew.
Dust was squeezed into solid rock.
Astronomers have named these rocky lumps
planetesimals.

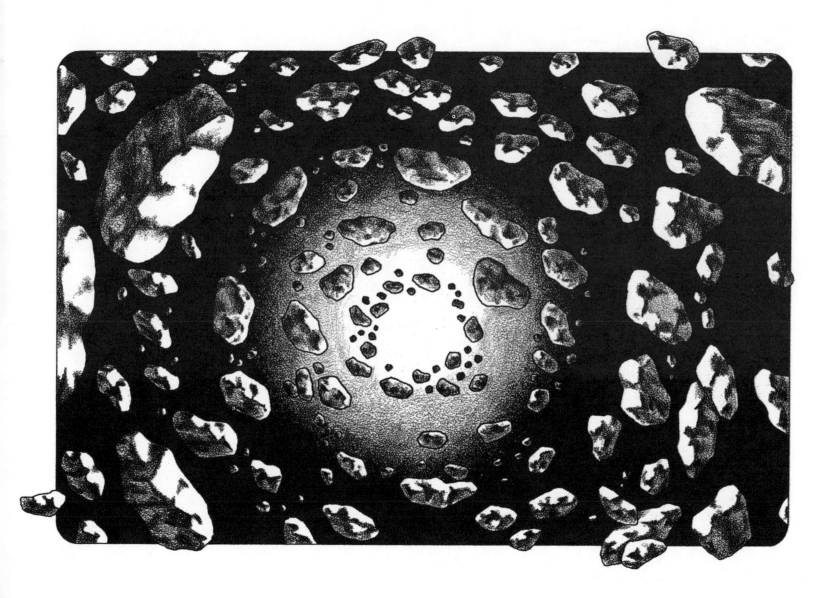

As they circled around
the core of hot gas,
the bigger planetesimals
swept up the smaller ones.
The biggest of these
became planet-sized.
Now some of these planet-sized
objects had smaller planetesimals
circling them!
In time, these smaller objects
would grow and become *moons*.

All this while, in the middle of the ring,
the core of hot gas was getting brighter.
Our Sun was being born.
Finally, after a hundred million years,
most of the planetesimals were gone.

In their place were
nine young planets.
At the center was one young sun.
Astronomers call this group
the *Solar System*.

Each planet
in the Solar System is different.
The planets nearest the Sun
are small and rocky and hot.

The ones farthest
from the Sun
are huge and covered
with poisonous gases.

In our solar system,
only one planet, Earth,
has the air and water
and warmth for things to live.
We are lucky.
Twenty billion years
after the big bang explosion,
we are the children
of the universe.
But who knows?
There may be life
in other parts of the universe.
Astronomers think
that it's likely.
There may even be
people like ourselves.

One thing is certain:
The universe sparkles on.
Now, as in the past,
fiery new stars are forming
even as we sleep.